# Friend(

## True Stories

*A Dolch Classic First Reading Book*

**by Edward W. Dolch and Marguerite P. Dolch**

**illustrated by Gary Undercuffler**

# The First Reading Books

The First Reading Books are fun reading books that fill the need for easy-to-read stories for the primary grades. The interest appeal of these true stories will encourage independent reading at the very beginning level.

The stories focus on the 95 Common Nouns and the Dolch Basic 220 Sight Vocabulary. Beyond these simple lists, the books use about two new words per page.

This series was prepared under the direction and supervision of Edward W. Dolch, Ph.D.

This revision was prepared under the direction and supervision of Eleanor Dolch LaRoy and the Dolch Family Trust.

## SRA/McGraw-Hill

A Division of The **McGraw-Hill** Companies

Original version copyright © 1958 by Edward W. Dolch.
Copyright © 1999 by SRA/McGraw-Hill. All rights reserved.
Except as permitted under the United States Copyright Act, no part of this publication may be reproduced or distributed in any form or by any means, or stored in a database or retrieval system without prior written permission from the publisher.

Printed in the United States of America.

Send all inquiries to:
SRA/McGraw-Hill
8787 Orion Place
Columbus, OH 43240-4027

ISBN 0-02-830797-6

4 5 6 7 8 9 0 QST 04 03 02 01

# Table of Contents

# Jet Liked to Play

Jet was a crow. Anika got him when he was a baby. Anika took good care of Jet. She gave him little pieces of hamburger to eat. Soon he was a big, black crow.

Jet played with Anika. Anika would hide her eyes. Jet would go and hide a little ribbon.

Then Jet would go back to Anika. Anika would try to find where Jet had put the ribbon.

As soon as Anika had found the ribbon, Jet would fly and get the ribbon and give it to Anika. But when Anika went to hide the ribbon, Jet would be looking to see where she put it. Anika could not get him to play the right way.

# Jet Goes for Help

Jet liked the girls who played with Anika. He liked to play with them, too. The girls said it was fun to play with a crow.

One day the girls said that they would like to go for a swim. The girls put on their swimsuits and went to the little river that was near the house. Jet went with them.

When Jet saw the girls go into the water, he cried, "Caw. Caw. Caw." He flew around and around over their heads. He did not want the girls to go into the water.

In every way that he could, Jet said that he wanted Anika and the girls to get out of the water.

The girls laughed at Jet. They were having a good time. They played in the water. At last, Jet flew away.

Jet flew right back to the house. He found Mother in the garden.

"Caw. Caw. Caw," said Jet.

Mother talked to Jet and wanted to play with him. But Jet did not want to play.

"Caw. Caw. Caw," said Jet.

Jet flew about Mother's head. Then Jet flew away. Then he flew back. He did this over and over. At last, Mother knew that Jet wanted her to go with him.

Jet flew right to the little river. Mother went with him. Mother was afraid that something had happened to Anika and the girls.

When Mother got to the river, the girls were having fun in the water.

Jet flew over the head of Anika. "Caw. Caw. Caw," said Jet. Jet was afraid that the water was going to hurt Anika.

Anika got out of the water. She put out her hand. Jet sat on her hand. He was very happy to see that Anika was out of the water.

Mother told Anika what Jet had done to get her to come down to the river.

Mother and Anika talked to Jet.
And they showed Jet what fun it was to
play in the water.

At last Jet was not afraid of the
water. He saw that the water would not
hurt Anika. Now when Anika and the
girls put on their swimsuits and go down
to the little river to swim, Jet goes, too.
He likes to play in the water with them.

# The Blue Jay

A robin had made a nest in a tree. One day, an owl came to the tree. The mother robin was afraid that the owl would find her nest. The owl might take the baby robins from the nest.

The robin flew around and around the owl's head. She cried and cried, but the owl did not move.

Then a blue jay flew to the tree. The blue jay flew at the owl and hit the big bird. The owl wanted to get away. But the owl could not see very much in the daytime. Owls see well at night.

Again the blue jay flew at the owl. The blue jay hit the owl again and again. The owl fell out of the tree to the ground. It went away to hide. Mother robin knew that the owl would not find her babies that day. She went back to the nest to keep her babies warm.

Sometimes a blue jay is not a very good bird. Sometimes a blue jay eats the eggs from the nests of other birds. But a blue jay does not go near a nest if the mother bird is sitting on the eggs.

All the birds know that the blue jay will fly at owls and squirrels. They know that the blue jay will let them know if owls or squirrels come near a nest. So the blue jay is like a police officer for the birds.

# Helping the Little Ones

Mother blue jay had three little baby birds in her nest. Day by day, Mother blue jay saw the babies grow and grow. At first, baby blue jays do not have any feathers. But at last they had their blue feathers and looked like little blue jays. It was time for them to fly. This is what happened to the baby blue jays.

Mother and Father got the babies out on a branch of the tree. The little birds moved their wings up and down.

Then, one fell from the branch and moved his wings just as if he were flying. He did not get hurt when he hit the ground.

Then another one went down, moving his wings. Then another one. The little blue jays found that they could move their wings and fly a little just like Mother and Father.

The little blue jays flew about on the ground. Mother and Father knew that something might hurt little birds on the ground, so they called from the tree. At last the little birds moved their wings and flew up to Mother and Father in the tree.

Every day the little blue jays flew more and more. One day, something funny happened to them. The little blue jays found a birdbath near the tree. There was water in the birdbath. The little birds played in the water. It was fun.

The three little birds got very wet in the water in the birdbath. From the birdbath, they flew down to the ground. Then they tried to fly up to the tree. They kept moving their wings up and down, trying and trying. But the little birds were very wet. Because of the water on their feathers, they could not fly up into the tree.

Mother and Father called and called, but the little birds could not fly up. Mother and Father saw that the little birds could not fly up to them. Then they did a very funny thing.

14

Mother and Father flew down to the ground and called, "Try. Try again. Try again."

One little blue jay tried to fly up. He got off the ground. Then Mother flew up under him. With the little blue jay on her back, she flew up into the tree.

Father called, "Try again. Try again." Another little bird tried to fly up into the tree. Father flew up under him and carried him up into the tree, just as Mother had done.

Mother came down and got the last little bird up on her back. Soon all three little birds were up in the tree. Father and Mother were happy to have their babies up in the tree again.

Mother sat in the tree and showed the little ones the way to get the water out of their feathers.

After that, when the little birds took a bath, they could get their feathers dry.

# A Funny Nest

It had rained all day. The wind blew. It blew so hard that a tree by the house was blown down.

Mother and Marcus heard the big noise, but the wind and rain blew so hard they could not go out. They were happy when they heard Father at the door.

"Are you all right?" called Father. "The tree by the house has blown down."

The rain had stopped. Mother and Marcus and Father went out to see the tree.

"We heard the big noise," said Mother, as they looked at the tree.

"Look. Look," said Marcus. "There is a bird's nest on the grass."

"The wind must have blown the bird's nest from the tree," said Father.

"Look," said Mother, "there are two baby robins in the nest."

"They are cold and wet," said Marcus. "Let us take the baby robins into the house where it is warm."

Marcus took the baby robins into the house. He took a strainer and in it made a nest for the robins. The robins were warm and dry.

Soon the baby robins wanted something to eat.

"What do baby robins eat?" said Marcus.

"We can give them little pieces of hamburger," said Mother. "But you will have to put it into their mouths."

Marcus put little pieces of hamburger into the mouths of the baby robins. Soon the babies were not hungry anymore. They were sleepy. They went to sleep that night in their strainer nest.

In the morning, the sun came out. Marcus went out to look at the big tree that had blown down.

"Mother, Mother," called Marcus. "The mother robin has come back. She is flying around the tree. She is looking for her nest. She is looking for the baby robins."

Mother and Father went out. They watched the mother robin flying around the tree.

"We must give the baby robins back to their mother," said Father.

"But there is no nest for the robins," said Mother.

"I have made a nest for the baby robins," said Marcus. "I made them a nest in a strainer."

"We can put the strainer on a branch in the tree," said Mother. "We can put the baby robins in the strainer. Then the mother robin might come back to her babies."

Father carried the strainer to a branch in a tree that was near the one that had blown down.

Marcus was very careful. He put
the baby robins in the nest that he had
made in the strainer.

The mother robin came back to
her baby robins. She took care of her
baby robins in the funny nest that
Marcus had made in the strainer.

# A Talking Bird

Mr. and Mrs. Yashima found in Malaya a mynah bird that they called Raffles. He was a very little baby bird.

Mrs. Yashima put the little bird in a cage. She took him with her on the boat to America.

Raffles did not like to be too hot or too cold. Mrs. Yashima had to be very careful of her mynah bird.

There was one thing that Raffles liked very much. He liked to take a bath. On the big boat to America, Raffles took a bath every day.

Mrs. Yashima had a cabin, a little room, on the boat. Every day Mrs. Yashima took Raffles out of his cage. She let him fly all around the cabin.

Every day Mrs. Yashima got warm water for Raffles. "Take a bath. Take a bath," said Mrs. Yashima.

Raffles would put one foot into the water. If the water was too cold, Raffles would not take a bath. If the water was too hot, Raffles would not take a bath.

"Take a bath. Take a bath," said Mrs. Yashima.

If the water was just right, Raffles would get into it. How Raffles liked to play in his bath water.

# What Raffles Said

Mrs. Yashima knew that a mynah bird was a talking bird. She wanted Raffles to talk to her, but Raffles would not say a thing.

One morning, just as Raffles was having a bath, Mrs. Yashima heard the bell for everyone to come out of their cabins onto the deck of the boat. Mrs. Yashima put Raffles in his cage and took him on deck.

On deck there was a man who was very cross. He had been sleeping in the sun when he heard the bell. He was sleepy and cross. He was talking to all the people about it.

Then Raffles looked at the cross man who was making so much noise.

"Take a bath. Take a bath," called Raffles.

All the people laughed and laughed.

Raffles was on many shows. He could say many things. All the people who saw Raffles said that he was the smartest bird they had ever seen.

# Gertie Makes a Nest

Gertie was a mallard duck. A mallard lives near water in the woods. But Gertie did not make her nest in the woods. She made her nest near a bridge in the city of Milwaukee.

One day, a man who was on the bridge saw three eggs on the top of a post called a pile. The man told the bridge keeper that a bird had made her nest on top of a bridge pile near the water.

The bridge keeper watched. Pretty soon he saw a mallard duck come to the pile. She sat on the eggs. He watched the duck take out some of the wood at the top of the pile. He watched the duck take out some of her feathers to make the nest bigger. When the duck flew away, there were four eggs in the nest on the top of the pile.

The bridge keeper called the duck Gertie. The bridge keeper talked to the newspaper. He said that a mallard duck had made a nest on top of a bridge pile. No one had ever heard of a mallard making a nest in a big city like Milwaukee.

The newspaper told all about Gertie making her nest on top of the pile and showed a picture of Gertie sitting on her nest.

The people of Milwaukee wanted to see Gertie. Many, many people went over that bridge every day. Everyone wanted to stop to see Gertie. A police officer had to come to the bridge to keep people moving.

The police officer looked after Gertie all the time she was on her nest. If Gertie was afraid, she might fly away and not come back again.

Every day the newspaper told about Gertie. More and more people heard about the duck that made her nest on top of a pile near a bridge in a big city.

More and more people came down to the bridge to see Gertie sitting on her nest. The police officer kept the people moving and quiet on the bridge. A man came all the way from Washington to see her. He wanted to see the mallard that would make a nest in a big city.

At last there were six eggs in Gertie's nest, and Gertie sat on her eggs to keep them warm.

All the people who went over the bridge tried to be quiet. They did not want Gertie to get off her nest.

Gertie knew just what she must do. She sat on her nest to keep her eggs warm.

# Gertie and the Ducklings

At last, one little duckling hatched out of its egg. The bridge keeper called him Long Bill because his bill was very long.

The newspaper showed a picture of Long Bill sleeping on Gertie's back.

Soon it took two police officers to keep all the people moving and quiet on the bridge. Everyone wanted to see Gertie and Long Bill.

Long Bill did not want to stay on Gertie's back. He wanted to move around. Gertie tried to make him stay under her in the nest until the other ducklings hatched, but Long Bill did not want to stay under Gertie.

There was not much room in the nest. One day, Long Bill fell out of the nest. He fell into the river. Gertie did not know what to do. Gertie knew that she must keep the eggs warm in her nest so that they would hatch, but she wanted to get Long Bill from the water.

At last Gertie got off her nest and flew down to get Long Bill. But Gertie could not carry the duckling back to the nest.

The police officers on the bridge did not know what to do. The people on the bridge did not know what to do.

The bridge keeper had to help Gertie. He got his boat and went after Bill. He caught Long Bill and put him back in Gertie's nest.

All the people on the bridge were happy.

Pretty soon Gertie had six little ducklings in her nest. Gertie was a good mother trying to take care of her babies.

Every day the ducklings were bigger. People took many pictures of them.

One day, it started to rain. It rained and rained. And the wind blew. Gertie sat on her nest on top of the bridge pile. It was hard to keep her six little ducklings dry.

Then Long Bill fell into the river.
Gertie flew down to the river to look for
Long Bill.

The five little ducklings in the nest
were wet and cold. They wanted their
mother. One by one, the five little
ducklings fell into the river.

The bridge keeper saw what was
happening. He got two friends to help
him. They got their boat. They found

Long Bill. They got four other ducklings out of the river, but they could not find one little duckling.

The five little ducklings were wet and cold. The bridge keeper put Gertie and the ducklings in a box. He put the box in his little house on the bridge. All night long, he kept them warm.

In the morning, Gertie and the ducklings were all right. The bridge keeper let them have some bread and milk. But the bridge keeper did not put them back into the nest. He did not want them to fall into the river anymore.

# Where Did Gertie Go?

There was a big store in Milwaukee. This big store had many big windows. The man who owned the store said that Gertie and her ducklings could stay in one of his big windows.

The man who owned the big store knew that many people would come to see Gertie and her ducklings in his store window.

He made one of the big windows look like the woods. There was water for the ducks to swim in. There were little trees and grass.

The man at the store took Gertie and the ducklings to the big store window. They lived in the store window. They liked it very much. They liked to swim in the water. They liked to sit in the grass.

Soon the street by the store was full of people who came to see Gertie and her ducklings. Police officers had to get the people out of the street so the cars could go by.

The man was afraid that the people would break the big window and be hurt. Police officers had to keep the people away from the window.

The man who owned the store said, "We must take Gertie and the ducklings away from here."

One morning, some men put Gertie into a box. They put the ducklings into another box. They put them into a car. And they took Gertie and the ducklings to a park where there was some water.

At the park, the men put the ducklings on the grass. The ducklings did not know what to do. Then the men took Gertie out of the box.

Gertie flew right to the water. She called to the ducklings. They all went to the water for a swim.

One day the man at the park caught Gertie. He wanted to put a band on her leg to show that she lived in the park. On Gertie's leg, the man found a band that said Gertie had been hatched in that very park. That might be why Gertie wanted to live in the city of Milwaukee. That might be why she made her nest by the bridge.

When the ducklings got bigger the men at the park put bands on their legs to show that they had been hatched in the city of Milwaukee, too.

Gertie and her ducklings were very happy at the park.

| | | | |
|---|---|---|---|
| a | bridge | everyone | hatch |
| America | but | eyes | hatched |
| about | by | fall | have |
| afraid | cabin | father | having |
| after | cabins | feathers | he |
| again | cage | fell | head |
| all | called | find | heads |
| an | came | first | heard |
| and | can | five | help |
| Anika | car | flew | helping |
| another | care | fly | her |
| any | careful | flying | here |
| anymore | carried | foot | hide |
| are | carry | for | him |
| around | cars | found | his |
| as | caught | four | hit |
| at | caw | friends | hot |
| away | city | from | house |
| babies | cold | full | how |
| baby | come | fun | hungry |
| back | could | funny | hurt |
| band | cried | garden | I |
| bands | cross | gave | if |
| bath | crow | Gertie | in |
| be | day | Gertie's | into |
| because | daytime | get | is |
| been | deck | girls | it |
| bell | did | give | its |
| big | do | go | jay |
| bigger | does | goes | jays |
| Bill | done | going | Jet |
| bird | door | good | just |
| birdbath | down | got | keep |
| birds | dry | grass | keeper |
| bird's | duck | ground | kept |
| black | duckling | grow | knew |
| blew | ducklings | had | know |
| blown | ducks | hamburger | last |
| blue | eat | hand | laughed |
| boat | eats | happened | leg |
| box | egg | happening | legs |
| branch | eggs | happy | let |
| bread | ever | hard | like |
| break | every | has | liked |

39

likes
little
live
lived
lives
long
look
looked
looking
made
make
makes
making
Malaya
mallard
man
many
Marcus
men
might
milk
Milwaukee
more
morning
mother
mother's
mouths
move
moved
moving
Mr.
Mrs.
much
must
mynah
near
nest
nests
newspaper
night
no
noise
not
now
of

off
officer
officers
on
one
ones
onto
or
other
out
over
owl
owls
owl's
owned
park
people
picture
pictures
pieces
pile
play
played
police
post
pretty
put
quiet
Raffles
rain
rained
ribbon
right
river
robin
robins
room
said
sat
saw
say
see
seen
she
show

showed
shows
sit
sitting
six
sleep
sleeping
sleepy
smartest
so
some
something
sometimes
soon
squirrels
started
stay
stop
stopped
store
story
strainer
street
sun
swim
swimsuits
take
talk
talked
talking
that
the
their
them
then
there
they
thing
things
this
three
time
to
told

too
took
top
tree
trees
tried
true
try
trying
two
under
until
up
us
very
want
wanted
warm
was
Washington
watched
water
way
we
went
were
wet
what
when
where
who
why
will
wind
window
windows
wings
with
wood
woods
would
Yashima
you